From a Stolen Time

FROM A STOLEN TIME

Selected Poems

Lana Wolkonsky

First Edition

All rights reserved, including the right of
reproduction in whole or in part in any form.

Copyright ©1998 by Lana E. Wolkonsky

Manufactured in the United States of America
ISBN:0-9653306-6-4

Library of Congress Catalog Card No.:98-090190

Dedicated to patience, compassion
and the storming will.

Table of Contents

Who Has a Life 11

Starting to Turn 12

Adored Darkness 13

Everybody's Share 14

Winged Spectator 15

In Fire's Eye 16

Free to Fall 17

Home the Road 18

One Morning 19

Walk 20

Un-Marked 21

Both in Toll 22

Prize a Day 24

Every Night 25

Telling Gestures 26

Hard Mechanics 27

Liquid Days 28

Reluctant Passage 29

On Ledge's Crossing 30

Time Lingers On 32

Notice Payed 34

On Latent Ground 35

The Front 36

Cross My Soul 37

Undissolvable Offense 38

Guide Our Course 39

A Close to Folly 40

Fortress of Winter 42

Of Finished Sunlight 43

Another's Dawn 44

Dreams May Flow 46

Who Has a Life

A secret life which lives the
Only waking hours of a day—
To tranquil wishes and a mild
Repose, to soft sojourns and amber
Lawns of autumn's magic pleasures.

Cold, dark winds and sparkling lights
Of frosted night in city calm, a tamed
Still, and iron will, a slow evolving
Enterprise: these only choices
Volunteer themselves; they
Bring a warmth, they spill
A heated pleasure.

Born and lived, they live these
Honors wild and so who has a
Life beyond these fleshy walls,
Receive a call to patched
Relations and a torn soul.

Starting to Turn

As it turns every year on these certain
Occasions, on the cycle of nature's
Own call does a wintery rise fill the
Squired redemption of already full
Hollows and readied apparel of Fall.

Already it slipped from our grasp;
Our loosened, wet grips are weakened
Content, but the loss still pursues in the
Colors of magic that change our opinions,

Change to delight. The sorrow of passing
Can no longer plenish; the mood and the
Spirit lie void of a call, and only when
These first uncertain street corners start
Forming concrete, as reality stales.

Bow to perfection, recline in the
Void—when winter leaves bare all
A harmony call. As the colors of
Warmth fade to give us sweet joy, in

The sparkle of permanence, rises a depth.
While we wait with attention this trouble
May pass and in doing un-doable deeds

Do we crumble at sights like the loss
Of the leaves: in only transparency —
Nowhere to hide, bury the summer in
Soft, padded heat of the winter approaching.

Adored Darkness

An unknown sun, a lost time—
From where the light shown on
This desolate stare, in mornings
Gone to aged reason might have
Seen horizons once. Now a finish
Comes to tales and swollen promises
Deflate, as all a lost encounter pains,

As nights seem endless on this face;
Torn desires, passed torment—might
Have seen another time when smiles
Were innocent and bright, where
Breezes seemed forever gentle.

They lost their luster—those moonlit
Passages; they shine into a darkened
Soul; their only light burns eerie
Darkness on a sorrowing still. The
Homes are quiet, the lights are dim
And only cherished hours sparkle

In our ever-coveted night. A lost
Time drowns in murky waters, the
Slate horizon soothes all present
Lies and grasses motionless stand
Tall on nature's corners, fill my
Days with more adored darkness.

Everybody's Share

This scaled beach with scattered
Shells, the open ocean rolling in—
Each tide caresses then releases
Into all eternity a smile, raced across
In perfect foam, breezed in light and
Chosen for another day. Your heart
Was coarse, as so each hour subsided

To make unfair a judgment's false array;
Appealed and parceled like tomorrow's
Wind which tosses light along this
Colorless bank, which leaves me
Bare to soft observe, to test the
Timed fortune, missed lot.

Let them unravel scavengers' bits,
Let others now decipher what in
Passing said left miles of traces:
Look into eternity and think a
Thought for once; no meaning
In this enterprise, no saved
Reason teaches as a wised
Known guides endless promise
Down uncharted waters.

Winged Spectator

You are not mine—sweet, lone observer;
Where your pack has left, to parts beyond
And lost the road becomes in this deceiving
Warmth, on void-of-frost October's May.

You fly above and sit beside to ponder
Mysteries unsolved, unheard; and now
To me you sail anew with gilt wings,
With beaded eyes, with formidable
Talents stretched across this aqua fill.

Once perched in challenge, breeded
In a secret sand and nested lone beyond
The roughness of our common friend, our
Shared depth, our only quest unconquered.
In it rise your daily fare, as soft in artificial
Tanks we oft observe them, here their constant

Peril drives us to be hungry with a broader
Curiosity, a longer spell. Disappear over
The shadowed circle of the last night's
Moon and drive my crescent dreams
Away, when nights spent wakeful
Leave a timid shore untouched.

In Fire's Eye

What do you think, sweet
Entombed magnificence—
In earthly silence blessed,
Like water lilies on a perfect,
Tranquil bed; a liquid life reflects.

Your sleep is silent, sweet—
I'll never know or dream as
You, what wishes may it bring.
Your gentle pant and trilling snore
Are harmonies unknown before; there

In the wind of passing time does love
Sing pleasures to this familiar shore.
An island you may be to some, but
In our only closeness, your reluctant

Glance I keep; to all past promises—
For them I ever gently weep. Humble
Stranger, angel's feet: who walks so
Coarsely on a padded street; in fire's
Eye, in hallowed meet, where only

Strangers covet passing, fleeing
Knowledge. And then each other's
Wisdom may be mine for once, as in
That instant I reverse my course.

Free to Fall

I am simple like the eye
Which looks in innocence
And deeds each hollow hour,
As a mirrored life in littleness
Distressed and such formidable
Glories as the setting past on me
Pretends, fear stands lone in this
Forgiving, distant hour. Loose not

Sight of underestimation, travel on
A log of man, and man's mysterious
Unknown might bless another's
Supposition of the matters judged
By outward cause. We are free to
Fall—the nations turn on us and
Minimal protection leaves a nation
Bare as individual protectors fail.

Only one can ride this trail and
Only one we are; I am simple
As the eye which sees the soul
Outlined as you. I am simple
As you complex may be and
So in simpleness we chart
Confusion lest it takes us
First; then fist-it-out, then
To another plain depart.

Home the Road

The grave stands still, the
Turquoise house, the missing names
There on the tombstone written.
Still the bark of now-dead Mars
Rings loud beyond the steel fence
As silent hallways' Venetian lamps
Still in their colors hang: bright orange,
Yellow, blue. And music sounds from
Every room; the cement garden paved
Gives way to shelled roses ever-prickle,
Birches, lilac, big tomatoes—still the taste
And Spring's aromas loud as neighbor's
Children laughter spill across the yard.

An old jalopy, light blue Delta 88
Now drives the ghost of Papa's smile
Around, it backs into the rotting wood
Telephone pole on Ocean Avenue each
Morning, then goes to check the mail in
Numbered boxes lost, buys the paper,
Gets the milk and only those old cartons
Changed. My heart bleeds wild, it misses
Every moment—to be a child again would
Be such perfect glory: when the world seemed
Big, when life was mine, when home the
Road was always open, where the bed was
Made if you had made it and a time stands still.
The nights I dream it over, lash on me a tender
Moment and my heart does breathe again.

One Morning

Earth and sky, land and sea—
All that a moment's enchantment
Can be, is a mere verse away, are
Daylights astray in the eerie green
Darkness of love's own, dear ways.

The magical forests, their tragic
Appeal are stretched-out before
Me, in that shadowed sun which
Casts lone forgiveness, and ever-
Appeasing the morning is mine
When ocean's a blanketed rug
To the north, when armies will
Fight with medieval valor.

The fences which bar glossy
Grasses from trees, fertile the
Grounds of this intimate key;
A groomed, shallow lawn and
Children's correction on love as
On earthly possession's recall.

Walk

Alone, in the barren land—
Of no sons, where the colors
Sparse, jump-out from a black
Earth; cover the blanket of red,
Slippery leaves and the smell
Of wet soil, my soil of country's
Lost forgiveness, a million times
Over. These naked branches reach

Into a clouded grey sky; as grey as
Years show in my stranger's bristles
And parched lips, as these grasses
Lie patted down by wetness. I walk
To a vulnerable shore, I seek the
Givings of a forgotten land, I sing
Internally. The sounds may only
Take away from this wild beauty

Seen on these Northeastern shores,
Abandoned till a new spring; left
To rot, to roar. Walk a venerable
Death, a quiet call: seek in love
These solemn trepidations and
Let my spirit loose, free; give for
Let, as shining rays a distance pass.

Un-Marked

If there was an empty space in the
Heart of time, to understand each
Moment, the lines of the earth
Would be certain, and weak (by
The days as the hours) a cry of

Lost sorrows would sound. The
Tenses of life also change, the
Strands of these passes are feeble
And gains seem to fall on most

Places; the remnants of past life
Still stand like museums in some
Rooms, and objects that given
With all of eternity taken, do also
Stand this lifetime un-marked.

Both in Toll

I lost you in the pink sunset,
In the haze of time, in the
Confusion of another world—
Of war, of righteousness, of
Longing. No child is this,
Who worthy of another
Cause does lie, no
Sibling spared in
Night's sweet
Torment;

I am the lonely bounty
Who must pay life's
Toll and lost your
Countenance; may
Be for now, but
So forever will
Accounted be
This love.

You live in pride
And pride may
Hold you back;
So loose yourself
Again, as bombs
Led back, as
Victories

Forever challenged
And our will shall
Never end until the
Last of battles fought
Shall find us both in toll.

Your face is never in surrender
And fight alone you still might
Do; so rise into your many spheres
And keep your judgments small—
I die without this pride and
Always knowing swallow life.

Prize a Day

The light everlasting, which
Shines across the tips of these
Trees; adorned in autumn's bounty—
Eternally appraised for endless time:
They give us our New York and every
Chilled moment warms again in this
Perfection, in an afternoon sun, in
A shadowed light. Soon they too,

Transparent will become and through
Their now-opulent leaves, a city bare
Will look: at us in cleaned, glass windows,
Gazing over park's splendour, winter whiteness
Looks; it pierces our staging. Now soft enjoy,

Today a quiet moment, brisk winds and
Fighting elements will win to prize a day
In England or in France: no trade for our
Sweet America, our freedom's painted
Pleasures. Today's uneven rug of
Tapestry's delight, a harmony

In colors only nature chose—
We hailed group of earthly
Visitors amaze this seasoned
Planting and a brush casts paint
Illusive on prized vision bright.

Every Night

The sky I grab in these last, colored rays;
In moments—each so varied in display,
In stroke, in light positions of the stars,
In painted beauty different every night;
Blueprint skyline charted, drawn on this
Now-speckled, silken sheet of delicate
Material: magical, ethereal; its touch
Is smooth across the palette of the eye
And my awaiting temper does not move
To raise the one already long-deciphered

Question. Mysteries undone—where does
This wonder end or start and so should we
As all, forget this choosing; only to remain
Eternal grants of life, a foiled appreciation
And an artist's touch, every night. Yes, it is
Such—these delicate amazements do not stop
To watch the ruin of a manly masquerade or
Liar's bluff; we wait in pain, in aging torment

Joy receive and shine our happy words on
Each without subjection to the petty scrutinies
Which all at once endured. Small we become
In front of this enormous sky of stars and virtue,
We raise the light magnificent; we mourn it in
Our artificial woes. Watch now, outside our
Covered worlds, to see the spectrum of relief
In beauty most unreachable in mysteries untold.

Telling Gestures

The roughness charm—
The best of hell against
An innocence long gone,
Raised every morning with

A harshness never dulled, a
Mild repulsion, meek—
Now shows in evident,
Outstanding jest; when
Romance gone into an

Endless time, left only—
Tenderness is in a word,
Forgotten. A manner strong,
And quiet reserve are now
The leaders of these signs
Of waning care, of lessened

Love; kick far, leave us and
Make your power known in
Each of these such telling
Gestures. Who is not as
Guilty in this doing: do

Not pretend, who on a
Coarsened path does lend
An hour sore; maybe tender
Souls have walked this way
Before (in silence). Modern
Light, reserve has banished
And the deadened storm
Erupts to ashes lost.

Hard Mechanics

Who has been to the edge
To watch this cold storm
Present itself; who has been
To the tropical fronts, to wave
The winds farewell and seek a
Calmer life; who has passed
And dared, who tried every
Obstacle, who won none.

Who, left with nothing but
Himself, now reaches low
To fix this hard mechanics,
Who roams the night, the
Island left untouched, who
Cried and realized life, who
Lives with all these tries and
Still holds strong: who dies.

Liquid Days

They do well with me, I know it—
Till the last of moments, when a sleep
Appeals not savory or strong; as it does
To me, when haunting captures in a force
This loud, pushing presence, this need.
It strikes in awkward moments, chosen
Not, and still (as still as night itself) it
Forces, as it is a force, to be expressed
In painful remedies, in short expulsion,
In a word. That silenced era gone—

There's left a one, lone melody: a
Melody of stars and now my pageant
Low brings heated compromise to
Trust. Enabled from the start, a
Stretch of joy unique can fix the
Most unfixable, as this floor
Presses up against me, I submit
To angels' calling and reverse
The praise. A fine humility has
Seen some better days; the music
Plays and liquid days go by.

Reluctant Passage

Colors fade and cold sets in,
As we are left with arrogant
Smiles, a few closed thoughts;
Eternally so challenged by
Sweet memories, by claiming
Histories, by closets full of
Unattained hope. Ours are

The hurtful charms, passioned
Lies with cradled songs that
Brought upon us such reluctant
Passage and an artful way of
Sought continuation. Rest

These muscles bare: now
Covered with a morning,
Dewful smile and loose the
Youth again, as over every day
These shining deaths do pass.

On Ledge's Crossing

Fragile life and timely days—
They see an outward longing
To reproach these rough,
Outnumbered prospects
Seen on scars of days,
On ledge's crossing.

This, the wintery feel,
Which now upon us in
Aggression seems, is
Caused through living,
Lashed on us in vain.

The skip, the harvest—
Sometime lost, the surface
Cast of splendid hopes and
Isolated dreams now rests with
Moons of previous redemptions.

On to lingering pains,
To petty torments, to a
Scattered world of friends,
In blanketed appeal—
So often resting.

Dash by fury's call and
Pass these storming worries,
That reveal us none; each tremble,
Each soft, vulnerable moment that
A breath is passed, that life may
Slip again from us; loose sight
Of passion's comment and
Bring up a thought instead!

Time Lingers On

Standing atop the blue, endless gulf—
The place he once stood, and we who
Looked in the eyes of timelessness,
Beauty, saw the abyss of perfection
Below, as he saw it. This, in his
Words was the final reflection,
The ultimate gesture, the flaw.

In the race of cool waters and
Romance, a song heard that
Echoed the hills; a fragrance,
A scene as the love chilled
By stalagmite caves, history's
Tales and the sound of a small
Motor running along the lagoon.

Still as the air in the night: fragrant
And lonely, I stand and I listen to
Quietly playing a tune once heard
Low in the streets of this port;
Later the ships brought us in.
History passed, index accumulate;
Lost and our dreams are just poor
Imitations. I walked in a daze, yet

Somehow the mirror of sadness now
Opened my soul and hardly exposed,
There the fear, there the plainness of
Accident felt; I was softly redeemed
By this madness; as often in life we
Are saved by our promises, saved
By the breath of our talents, our
Nature, and time lingers on.

Notice Payed

It may be just another day—
When aircraft disappear
Into the clouds and
Shrouded ignorance
Abides around. A
Day when notice
Payed to some is
Just a passing
Prejudice or
Flaring of
Some harsh,
Judgmental
Pride.

A tear falls soft for these
Unwilling souls who ride
Life dry and in a drunken
Purity call stark naïve
The caring lot. They
Are betrayed by
Lauding, laughter
And the sentiment
Of hate which
Tightened on
Their lips
Does never
Rest.

On Latent Ground

The long retreat of aging news,
Of lingering sadness, of a silent
Fall begets the cold, the wetness
Bare on branches now in color
So enhanced. Their yellows
Dulled, their mossy green
Appeal now fights out from
Their browned stems and we

Pass slow along this walkway
Chipping, waiting for another
Dawn of newness. In this final
Setting, winds have deadened;
Only this last turn before a
Winter silence lashes frozen
Praise on latent ground.

The Front

In all its madness, driving in—
A wall of rain is ours today
And tropics bend to serve
This will, of nature's
Force, of God's
Own skill.

We sit, we face an endless
Count upon a silvered
Screen: a world of
Diamond drops that
Stream beyond the
Dance of palms,
Now wild in

Rain. Their ecstasy
Is felt in every
Movement seen,
Unseen. As in our
Fragile lives, a

Human note to
Feelings touched—
By saddened phrase,
By lingering lot, a
Toughened call,
A broken charm.

Cross My Soul

Here my sweet heart sings a cry heard low
Across the land once prized, in soft refrains;
It agonizes harmonies and fills an overflowing
Heart to rest alone, as all a lone heart knows.

Take nothing in this heading rain, this cloud of
Storm which raises light along the battling shore
And note a maddening light, a freed emotion.
Sink now into sliding fear, a mighty stage
To once rehearsed appeal—now mine is
Void: I see your interest wane and find a sole
Amusement in the gentle interest, hearts of men.

So in my ways, when quiet nights abide, alone
I'll see the greying years in subdued lights and
Play the lowest cards in vain; when only those left
Pure will stand to meet my light in world's own ends,
In falling strains. Released into a time forgotten, worries
Then will fade to none, ashes cross my soul shall rest.

Undissolvable Offense

There are no victories today,
When justice passes on its
Own accord and buries
In the deep of winter's
Calling every plea.

Behind the hidden snows
A solitude still lingers
And in its stillness
All is found, as
Surface dust
May fall so
Trivial.

The dreams of night
Are cast in grey—
Articulate and
Punctuated, all
Life's stories go.

They disappear into the
Silence of a falling snow
And blend so purely with
An undissolvable offense—
In earnest quiet, on we go.

Guide Our Course

When there is quiet grey
Along a slate sky, when
In a moment's stillness
Life does lie and in itself
A pledge is made to honour
Trust that freely had been

Given out. A trust that
All-encompassed, loved;
That spoke the very words
Of love, yet in an instant
Could have broken, fallen
To the depths of sorrow.

Some inexplicable joy
Made it a whole, entire
And to these splendid
Wishes pass but dreams
On early afternoons of
Silence: when sounds
Of words need not
Express a blessing,

When movement calls
Alone its own sensation
And when a mere expression
Changes lives of words to
Troubleless, to free-of-effort
Thoughts that guide our course.

A Close to Folly

To ponder of those grey uncertainties,
Of hidden mysteries that only in
Tomorrow's promise hold a
Picture true, is to believe
That all our just foundation
May in time be crumbled
By this very time itself,
By saddened days, by
Night's own shadow.

In these sorry days to come, may we
Live out our distance in a modest
Light and all such modesties
May pass us too as we
Draw a close to folly,
As the light shines
Low, as vivid
Signs flash
Warning

On the frazzled shimmer seen in
Eyes of greed, blinded by their
Busyness, their moment.
When we go beyond
Our thoughtful
Dreams, our
Pensive

Moments, when the wandering stops,
When stays are frozen in our minds,
The tears of weeping mercy shed
On us and we, so proud,
Refuse the substance
Of our days.

Fortress of Winter

When there is nothing to do,
But a grey wall looks at me
In semi-distress, to appease
The unknown, to revive the
Enamored appeal of a Spring
Full and green; we've since
Long-forgotten, since lost,
Dismayed. Now in this

Fortress of winter remain
Such few glimpses of
Youth-fragrant skin, of the
Captured emotion that love
Once brought home. Sweet
Was the day when ardor
Once filled to the top of my
Stay; here in passed distress,
Here in pages now turned.

Of Finished Sunlight

Stream of light, this light of days
That pass in golden solitude, in
Aging, graceful hues that fall
Upon the earth; one such
Evening, when it spills
Into a mid-moon harvest,

Time aging shall never still
And those Sardinian afternoons—
As drenched in that most endless
Sun, a younger beauty walked.
And laughed with laughter now

Not known, with only appetites
Untouched through time, a
Summer may indeed be
Over many times again.

Listen for the distant sound
Of echoed children, of the
Dogs at dusk, of farms over
The hill, of finished sunlight
And a different moon each year.

Another's Dawn

In this endless winter, in the land of
False starts and truthless propositions,
Amid a falling nation as in the freezing
Rains, stand still sweet knowledge; let
Our horizons fade. Wake us when the

Power ends: the mirror shines a face
Dead; wish upon the morning's glory
Gone to southern shores, when we will
Hang free, when on our lips are written
Only notions and we awaken to an old

Friend, a passed enemy, a rival lesser
Than ourselves. Write me then to tell
Of why rejection passes; sing the softer
Tones in lashes sent across my scorched
Soul and let the accusations fall on me

Again. We loose not if once we lost
Ourselves, as in a quiet night (so many
Passed) our freed promises, our missed
Targets, our futures walk in front of us—
They have no time to see, to challenge

Us. So sleep the minute particle of
Life away and take the road home that
In another life was once decided closed;
Awaken only but to die a loss and there
To seek farewell in dreamed arms, in

Spirited attempt. Let legacy survive
These trivial passings and receive a
Harmony anew, while in the light of
Yet another's dawn, a shadow strides
With me—it is but vague reflections
Painted 'top a frozen, tearful sea.

Dreams May Flow

These are the thoughts
Now prevalent in mind's
Own forefront on an
Evening splendid,

Setting on tomorrow's
Bleak reflection, barely
Noticed, fadings of the
Past. Guiding to an
Open marker, staged

In light and tumbling
To a tearful ground—
There is no resolution
To the call of forces
Won. In this glass sea,
All seen, all blinded

By another time, lies
Still the common will,
The mundane corner,
Quiet for another day.
Until some foreign
Resonance is heard
And dashing in a

Windward snow
Along the pink
Horizon, dreams
May flow.

From a Stolen Time was designed at
The Oliphant Press, New York City, and
printed in an edition of five hundred copies.
The typeface used is Adobe Garamond. All
papers used in the book are recycled.